W9-AVM-228

LIFE WITH
SPINA BIFIDA

BY HEIDI AYARBE

Published by The Child's World®
1980 Lookout Drive • Mankato, MN 56003-1705
800-599-READ • www.childsworld.com

Content Consultant: Benjamin C. Warf , M.D., Professor of Neurosurgery, Harvard Medical School

Photographs ©: Wave Break Media/Shutterstock Images, cover, 1, 16; Shutterstock Images, 5; Jane Kalinowsky/AP Images, 6; Lenny Ignelzi/AP Images, 8; DGAA/ZDS/ Rocky/Wenn/Newscom, 11; Weekend Images Inc./iStockphoto, 12; iStockphoto, 15; Paul Crate/The News Chief/AP Images, 19; Bill Hughes/Bloomsburg Press Enterprise/ AP Images, 20

ISBN 9781503825161
LCCN 2017959684

Printed in the United States of America
PA02375

TABLE OF CONTENTS

FAST FACTS

- Spina bifida (SB) is a type of birth **defect**. The **spinal cord** is made up of nerve fibers. These nerves send messages as electrical signals between the brain and the rest of the body. When someone has SB, the person's spinal cord tissue and nerves have not formed the way they should. This can prevent the spinal cord and nerves from working properly.

- In the United States, approximately 166,000 people have SB.

- SB can be caused by a defect within a person's **genes**. SB may run in families. It often can be avoided if the mother takes extra **folic acid**.

- Abilities and disabilities among people with SB can vary greatly based on the location of the defect and the amount of nerve damage involved.

- Many people with SB also have hydrocephalus. Hydrocephalus is a condition in which fluid builds up and causes pressure in the brain.

- There is no cure for SB. Treatment varies from person to person but often includes surgery, medication, and adaptive equipment such as crutches to assist in mobility. Some people also benefit from physical and behavioral therapy.

THE NERVOUS SYSTEM

Spina bifida affects the body's nervous system. The nervous system is made up of the nerves, brain, and spinal cord.

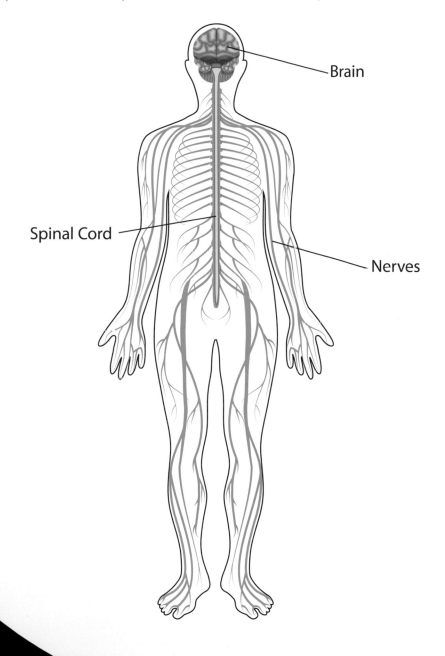

Brain

Spinal Cord

Nerves

Chapter 1

ROLLING WITH LIFE

Aaron Fotheringham spent hours watching his older brother, Brian, perform tricks in the neighborhood skate park on his racing bike. One afternoon, Brian took Aaron to a ramp that was 4 feet (1.2 m) high. Aaron guided his wheelchair to the edge, and his brother pushed him down. Aaron glided until his front wheels caught a ridge. He flew out of his wheelchair, skidding across the pavement.

Aaron pulled himself back into his wheelchair, his face and hands stinging from the impact. But the rush of the free fall made him wheel back up to the top of the ramp to try again. He was only eight years old at the time.

◀ **Aaron Fotheringham performs a trick at a skate park in 2007.**

▲ **Aaron practices a jump off a ramp in 2011.**

But on that day, extreme wheelchair skating was born. Aaron called the sport Hardcore Sitting.

Aaron was born with myelomeningocele (my-uh-loh-muh-NIN-guh-seel) SB, the most serious type of SB. He was adopted when he was a baby.

His adoptive parents received a phone call that there was a newborn in the hospital who needed a family. Aaron's parents brought him home when he was just a few weeks old.

Aaron has had many painful surgeries. These include surgeries on his **spinal column** and hips. Early in life, Aaron used crutches to get around. But using crutches could be painful and slow. By the time he was eight years old, Aaron had started using a wheelchair full-time.

TYPES OF SB

There are many types of SB. SB occulta occurs when there is a small gap in one or more bones of the spine, but the spinal cord and nerves form properly. Closed neural tube defects occur when there are defects in the fat tissue around the lower spinal cord. Meningocele SB occurs when spinal **membrane** and fluid protrude from an opening in the spine. Myelomeningocele SB occurs when part of the spinal cord and nerves are pushed through an opening in the spine. They form a fluid-filled sac. This type of SB often causes some degree of **paralysis**.

Aaron was hooked on the speed and freedom the wheelchair gave him.

Aaron loved the skate park. He practiced each trick hundreds of times, destroying wheelchair tires and rims. When he was 15, he landed the first-ever wheelchair backflip.

Aaron started competing in skateboarding and biking competitions. But instead of using a bike or board, he used his wheelchair. Today, Aaron is a professional Hardcore Sitter. He works as a stuntman and tours with Nitro Circus, a sports entertainment company that employs athletes who perform stunts. He also works at summer camps for kids who have disabilities, teaching them how to use their wheelchairs. Aaron continues to change the way the world views people with disabilities, one trick at a time.

Aaron tours the world and performs stunts with Nitro Circus. ▶

Chapter 2

FIRST DAY

Caitlin sat up in bed as her morning alarm beeped. Her stomach did flip-flops. It was her first day of middle school.

Caitlin pulled on the clean shirt and jeans she had laid out the night before. She scanned the calendar hanging on her wall, looking for the date and the color red. The tasks she'd marked in red were the most important. She'd written "first day of school" on today's date.

Caitlin was born with SB and hydrocephalus. Her hydrocephalus was treated with a shunt tube. This tube drained the excess fluid from her brain into her **abdomen**. From there, the fluid was absorbed naturally into her bloodstream.

◄ **People with SB who have trouble with memory and learning often use tools such as calendars to stay organized.**

CHIARI MALFORMATIONS

Some people with myelomeningocele SB have a type 2 Chiari malformation. When someone has this malformation, the cerebellum and brainstem are displaced below an opening in the skull where the spinal cord connects to the brain. The cerebellum is the part of the brain that controls balance and coordination. The brainstem helps control breathing, speaking, and swallowing. Brain development, as well as the functioning of the cerebellum and brainstem, may be affected in someone who has a type 2 Chiari malformation.

Caitlin also had been born with a type 2 Chiari (kee-AHR-ree) malformation. Because of this, she had some trouble with memory and learning. Her calendar was part of a plan developed by her organizational tutor, teachers, and parents. Her tutor helped her develop organizational skills.

SB did not visibly affect the use of Caitlin's legs, so it was not easy to tell she had SB. But she felt weak sometimes.

▲ **School-related or organizational tasks can be difficult for some people with SB.**

She often had trouble with bladder and bowel control. She had to manage her bathroom breaks by a schedule. She programmed her phone to set off alarm reminders. The reminders helped her remember to go to the bathroom and take her medications.

Each day, Caitlin worked with her organizational tutor. The tutor showed her how to use a calendar to organize her schoolwork and tasks by colors. This helped Caitlin know which subjects to study and in which order. Because of this, Caitlin was now ready for her first day of school. She smiled and shrugged on her backpack.

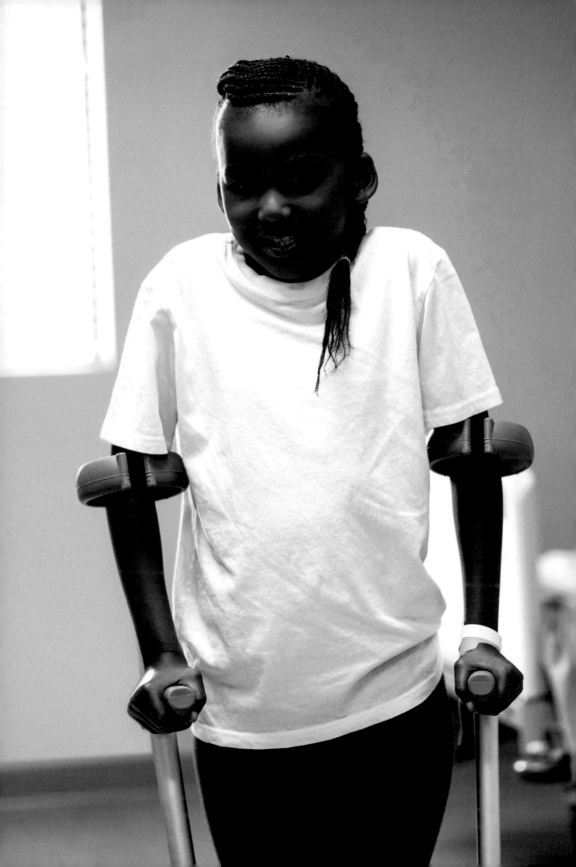

Chapter 3

OPENING NIGHT

Twelve-year-old Julia stood behind the curtain, waiting for her cue. She peeked out and saw a sea of faces in the audience. Her palms were sweaty. She wiped them on her thighs and held onto her crutches.

Last year, she would never have tried out for the school play. She was the only person in her school with SB. People often saw her disability instead of her. After a while, Julia started focusing on her disability and limitations, too.

When she was younger, Julia had written down a list of things she could not do. She could not walk without crutches. She could not participate in school sports such as the soccer team. She could not dance ballet.

◄ **Some people with SB use forearm crutches.**

But ever since Julia had gone to Camp Spifida last summer, she'd begun to think about her disability differently. Camp Spifida was a summer camp for kids with SB. The experience had helped her realize she was not alone. At camp, she was given choices of all the things she could do: canoeing, rafting, theater, and art. She had never felt so accepted. And tonight, she would show her acting skills to her school and community.

It was the opening night of the school musical. And Julia had landed the lead role. The role required the actor to be physically skilled. She would have to dance as well as sing.

At tryouts, Julia had impressed the director with all the tricks she could do with her crutches. Now, after weeks of practice, she was prepared and excited. The curtains parted. A hush fell over the crowd as Julia stepped into the spotlight.

Many sports, such as waterskiing, can be adapted for people ▶ who have SB.

Julia began to sing. Her voice filled the room. Piano music accompanied her from the orchestra pit below the stage. Other actors came out from behind the curtain and joined her. Julia saw her parents in the audience. They waved to her. She smiled. She had never felt so alive.

THINK ABOUT IT

- Some people with SB, such as Caitlin, have a type of disability that is often not visible. What health problems might a person with SB have that are invisible?
- Think about your favorite sport or activity. How might you adapt it for someone who has SB?
- How could you be a good friend to someone you know who has SB?

◀ Camp Spifida is a summer camp in Pennsylvania for children with spina bifida.

GLOSSARY

abdomen (AB-duh-muhn): The abdomen is the part of the body that contains the digestive organs, including the stomach and the intestines. Caitlin's shunt tube drained excess fluid from her brain into her abdomen.

defect (DEE-fekt): A defect is a physical problem that causes some part of the body to not work as it should. Spina bifida is a type of defect that occurs while the baby is growing inside the mother.

folic acid (FOH-lik A-syd): Folic acid is a vitamin that helps cells grow and develop. Extra folic acid in a mother's diet can help reduce the risk of having a baby with spina bifida.

genes (JEENZ): Genes are located within the body's cells, and they determine which traits are passed down to a child from the parents. Spina bifida can be caused by a defect in a person's genes.

membrane (MEM-brayn): A membrane is a thin layer of tissue that protects organs and other parts of the body. A membrane surrounds and protects the spinal cord.

paralysis (puh-RAL-uh-siss): Paralysis occurs when someone loses the ability to move part or all of the body. People with myelomeningocele spina bifida may have partial or full paralysis of the legs.

spinal column (SPY-nuhl KOL-uhm): The spinal column is the backbone, which protects the spinal cord. Some people who have spina bifida need surgery on their spinal column.

spinal cord (SPY-nuhl KORD): The spinal cord is a cord of nervous tissue, protected by the backbone, that is the messenger from the brain to the rest of the body. Someone who has spina bifida has an abnormally formed spinal cord.

TO LEARN MORE

Books

Gray, Susan H. *The Nervous System*. Mankato, MN: The Child's World, 2015.

Moss, Wendy. *The Survival Guide for Kids with Physical Disabilities & Challenges*. Minneapolis, MN: Free Spirit, 2015.

Poole, Hilary W. *Disability and Families*. Broomall, PA: Mason Crest, 2017.

Web Sites

Visit our Web site for links about spina bifida:

childsworld.com/links

Note to Parents, Teachers, and Librarians: We routinely verify our Web links to make sure they are safe and active sites. So encourage your readers to check them out!

SELECTED BIBLIOGRAPHY

Cornell, Marly. *The Able Life of Cody Jane: Still Celebrating*. Minneapolis, MN: LightaLight Publications, 2011.

"Spina Bifida." *Centers for Disease Control and Prevention*. U.S. Department of Health & Human Services, 2017. Web. 6 Aug. 2017.

"What Is SB?" *Spina Bifida Association of America*. Spina Bifida Association of America, 2015. Web. 8 Aug. 2017.

INDEX

ABOUT THE AUTHOR

Heidi Ayarbe is a writer, translator, and storyteller. She is a native of Nevada but now makes her home in Colombia, South America, with her husband and two daughters.